COUNT THE
POOPS, POOS & PLOPS!

WELCOME TO
COUNT THE POOPS, POOS & PLOPS!

GOOD LUCK!

Count the POOPS!

There are

3

POOPS!

COUNT the POOPY HEADS!

There are 5 POOPY HEADS!

WHICH POOP APPEARS THE MOST?

This POOP appears 8 times

This POOP appears 8 times

This POOP appears 9 times

SO this POOP...  appears the MOST!

COUNT THE **DRIVING** POOPS!
(but don't count the passenger poops!)

There are

8

DRIVING POOPS!

How many poops
are left to flush?

There are **12** POOPS left to **FLUSH!**

CHRISTMAS vs HALLOWEEN POOPS! Which appears the most?

There are **10** HALLOWEEN POOPS

and **8** CHRISTMAS POOPS

So there are more HALLOWEEN POOPS!

HOW MANY **POOPS AND PLOPS** CAN YOU **SPOT?**

There are **9** POOPS & PLOPS!

COUNT THE POOPS BEING **TAKEN ON A WALK!**

There are

5

POOPS BEING TAKEN
ON A WALK!

There are

6

STINKY POOPS!

WHICH **POOP** APPEARS THE **LEAST**?

This **POOP** appears **9** times

This **POOP** appears **8** times

This **POOP** appears **9** times

So this **POOP**...  appears the least!

COUNT the POOPS WITH HATS!

There are

POOPS
With HATS!

PLOPS WITH FEET...

How many can you spot here?

There are

11

PLOPS WITH FEET!

COUNT THE DOODLE POOPS!

There are **10** DOODLE POOPS!

COUNT THE
PIRATE POOPS!

There are

4

PIRATE POOPS!

COUNT the BABY POOPS!
(they're green!)

There are

8

BABY POOPS!

HAPPY vs UNHAPPY POOPS ...

WHICH OF THEM APPEARS THE MOST?

There are **10** HAPPY POOPS

and **10** UNHAPPY POOPS

So there are the **same amount** of both!

How many poops have glasses?

There are

7

POOPS WITH glasses!

THE END!

Find us on Amazon!

Discover all of the titles available in our store; including these below...

I SPY
EVERYTHING!

I SPY
ANIMALS!

I SPY
FROM A-Z!

I SPY
IN THE CITY!

I SPY
AT THE SEASIDE!

I SPY
IN THE COUNTRYSIDE!

Printed in Great Britain
by Amazon